MINI

Gillian Bardsley

SHIRE PUBLICATIONS

Published in Great Britain in 2013 by Shire Publications Ltd, Midland House, West Way, Botley, Oxford OX2 0PH, United Kingdom.

43-01 21st Street, Suite 220B, Long Island City, NY 11101, USA.

E-mail: shire@shirebooks.co.uk   www.shirebooks.co.uk

A CIP catalogue record for this book is available from the British Library.

Shire Library no. 757.   ISBN-13: 978 0 74781 255 5

Gillian Bardsley has asserted her right under the Copyright, Designs and Patents Act, 1988, to be identified as the author of this book.

Designed by Myriam Bell Design, UK and typeset in Perpetua and Gill Sans.

Printed in China through Worldprint Ltd.

13 14 15 16 17   10 9 8 7 6 5 4 3 2 1

COVER IMAGE
Publicity for the Morris Mini-Minor in 1961 (see page 19).

TITLE PAGE IMAGE
A Mini Mark III, painted in patriotic Union Jack colours, is pictured in front of another British icon, Tower Bridge in London.

CONTENTS PAGE IMAGE
A Morris Mini Cooper 'S' Mark II from 1968 with two young women wearing that symbol of the 'Swinging Sixties', the mini-skirt.

ACKNOWLEDGEMENTS
I would like to thank the British Motor Industry Heritage Trust for their generous support in preparing this work and Colin Corke for his invaluable assistance in researching the text and images.

The images in this book are drawn from the unique photographic collections of the BMIHT. Many were taken by the talented in-house photographers who worked at the Longbridge and Cowley factories. I am grateful to the Issigonis estate for their permission to reproduce the pictures on page 5 from their personal collection and to John Baker (www.austin-memories.co.uk) for permission to reproduce the picture on page 54. The picture on page 53 was taken by the author.

Shire Publications is supporting the Woodland Trust, the UK's leading woodland conservation charity, by funding the dedication of trees.

CONTENTS

WHERE IT ALL BEGAN

THE MINI IS UNUSUAL for being closely associated with one individual in an industry whose products are usually the result of complex, and largely anonymous, teamwork. Yet the name of Sir Alec Issigonis is still recognised, for he was possibly the British motor industry's first and only celebrity.

His future status as the creator of a British icon, epitomising the 'youth' culture which dominated the 1960s, was not obvious in his origins. Alexander Arnold Constantine Issigonis was born on 18 November 1906 in the busy Turkish port of Smyrna (now called Izmir). He was the only child of Constantine Issigonis, a marine engineer of Greek origin, and his wife, Hulda, who belonged to a German brewing family. Despite their ancestry, both his parents were born and raised in Turkey, but to complicate things further, they were also staunch Anglophiles. Constantine had spent some time in England as a young man and been given British citizenship. So young Alec was given a private English education and instilled with loyalty to a country that he had not had the opportunity to visit.

Alec Issigonis, Morris Motors project engineer, at Cowley in 1946. This was the period during which the Morris Minor, which established his reputation, was being designed.

The comfortable way of life enjoyed by Smyrna's expatriate community was rudely shattered by the First World War in which Turkey chose the losing side. As a consequence, international war was followed by civil war, and in 1922 the Royal Navy arrived to evacuate the British community. While they waited on Malta as refugees, Constantine fell gravely ill and died. Hulda and her son, now sixteen years old, crossed to Sicily and travelled the length of Europe to reach their new home in England.

Here Issigonis resumed his education, completing an engineering diploma at Battersea Polytechnic in 1928 and gradually making his way into the motor industry. Though the British economy was struggling during this period, the motor car had only been invented around forty years previously, and the industry which had grown up around it proved more resilient than many older sectors. In 1936 Issigonis was offered an opportunity as a suspension designer with Morris Motors, one of the leading motor manufacturers of the time, based at Cowley near Oxford. Two years earlier, the firm's founder, William Morris, had been created Lord Nuffield in recognition of his great philanthropy.

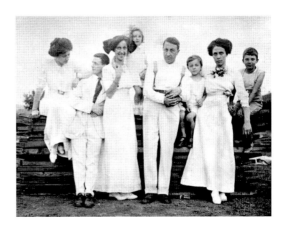

Constantine, Alec and Hulda Issigonis are fifth to seventh from left in this picture, together with their extended family in Turkey, c. 1910.

As his career began to take off, Issigonis dedicated his leisure time to motor sport, modifying a series of Austin Sevens. He spent much time both as competitor and spectator at racing circuits and hill-climbs. In 1934 he began work with his friend, George Dowson, to construct an innovative racing car completely from scratch. The resulting 'Lightweight Special' took five years to build entirely by hand and began to compete in 1938. Motorsport was suspended for the duration of the war from 1939, but the car returned once peace was established, and enjoyed several more years of successful competition before Issigonis and Dowson retired from the amateur racing scene in 1948.

With the outbreak of the Second World War, Issigonis, as part of a reserved occupation, was officially assigned to the design of military vehicles. At the same time, the vice-chairman of Morris Motors, Sir Miles Thomas, encouraged him to work on ideas for a new small car. Though production and design of civilian vehicles was banned until 1944, most motor manufacturers continued to work discreetly on post-war designs in the hope that they could gain an advantage over their rivals when the war was over.

Alec Issigonis, driving his modified Austin Seven Sports near his home in Purley, Croydon, c. 1930.

Left: Issigonis designed and built the Lightweight Special in his spare time. It enjoyed considerable competition success in the late 1940s and taught him much about car design.

Right: As part of the war effort, Issigonis designed an amphibious motorised wheelbarrow to be airlifted to troops in the field. In 1944, he tested it for himself on the lake at Blenheim Palace in Oxfordshire.

So, alongside armoured cars and motorised amphibious wheelbarrows, Issigonis and his small team worked away on the 'Mosquito' project which was well advanced as the end of hostilities approached in 1945. The Mosquito was launched as the Morris Minor at the London Motor Show in October 1948. The American-influenced styling of this small car was strikingly modern, while it set new standards for its use of space, its pioneering rack-and-pinion steering and excellent suspension. It also featured remarkably small wheels, a repeating theme in Issigonis's future work. As a result, its handling and ride were impressive for a car of its size. The Morris Minor's unusual appearance provoked strong antipathy from Lord Nuffield, who likened the car to a 'poached egg' but the buying public disagreed with him. The car was a great success and was an important step towards establishing Issigonis as a leading British designer.

In 1952, however, strong overseas competition prompted Morris Motors to conclude a merger with its chief rival, the Austin Motor Company, which was based at Longbridge near Birmingham. The outcome was the formation of the British Motor Corporation (BMC). Issigonis shied away from the in-fighting which commonly accompanied such reluctant unions. He therefore decided to move to the smaller, Coventry-based firm

This picture was taken outside the camouflaged Morris Motors factory at Cowley in 1944. Issigonis led a small team working on the Mosquito prototype alongside the 'official' war-time projects.

Lord Nuffield looks unenthusiastically under the bonnet of the recently launched Morris Minor in 1948. Four years later he would agree to the merger with Austin that created the British Motor Corporation.

of Alvis, where his brief was to design a luxury 8-cylinder car codenamed TA/350. During his three-year tenure at Alvis, he developed new ideas and formed relationships that would be important in his future career. As well as new work colleagues, he began his collaboration with suspension designer Alex Moulton. The TA/350 never went into production because, by 1955, Alvis had decided it was too great a risk for them to produce an expensive new model, which they feared would not appeal to their conservative customer base. By coincidence, at this very moment the chairman of BMC, Sir Leonard Lord, was looking for an innovative designer to move BMC forward. Issigonis was offered the post of deputy engineering director and returned not to Cowley, but to Longbridge, with its superior technical facilities entirely at his disposal. The story of the 'Mini' was about to unfold.

A sketch by Issigonis of the Alvis TA/350, c. 1952, incorporating the distinctive Alvis triangle badge on the bonnet.

In recent years there has been a significant trend in the development of small cars. As one of the world's largest manufacturers of small and medium sized cars, the British Motor Corporation have now, after intensive research, produced an entirely new concept in small car design.

In times past, a small car was designed as a cheap expedient to reach the person who could not afford to buy or run a bigger car. However, to negotiate to-day's congested streets in the cities of the world, the small car has become a necessity. It is for this reason that B.M.C. designers have concentrated their efforts on producing a car of compact exterior dimensions, yet with maximum room and comfort *inside* for four adults. How well they have achieved their objective, and how many revolutionary new features have been evolved in so doing, can be judged from a careful examination of the end product — the incredible new Austin Seven.

The whole world demands thi

OUT OF AUSTERITY

T HE BRIEF given to Issigonis when he arrived at Longbridge towards the end of 1955 was not, however, to produce a new small car. Len Lord wanted a family of advanced-technology vehicles to inject some excitement into the ageing model range that BMC had inherited from both Austin and Morris. Ironically, the Issigonis-designed Morris Minor was still one of the company's leading products, alongside the homely Austin A30/A35 and the stolid Austin Cambridge and Morris Oxford. While Lord waited for results, he called in the Italian styling house of Pininfarina – father Battista and son Sergio – who gave the existing model range a makeover. This resulted in the BMC Farinas, which began with the launch of the Austin A40 Farina in 1958, a reworked Austin A35, turning a traditional Austin product into an elegant fashion item. It was quickly followed by Farina versions of the Oxford, Cambridge and Westminster.

Opposite: The 1959 launch brochure for the Austin Seven (one of the names given to the two original versions of the Mini). BMC explains its rationale in producing such a ground-breaking small car, claiming 'the whole world demands this'.

Left: In September 1958 BMC launched the Austin A40 Farina outside the Longbridge Exhibition Hall. Left to right: chairman Leonard Lord, Italian stylist Battista Pininfarina, deputy chairman George Harriman, Sergio Pininfarina and (top right on the steps) Alec Issigonis.

A brightly painted mockup of XC9001 outside Longbridge's administration offices (known as the 'Kremlin') in 1956. Though it was a more conventional design, it foreshadows the future shape of the Mini.

Issigonis, meanwhile, began work on the new model range. He gathered round him a close-knit team of engineers comprising colleagues who had worked with him at Cowley on the Morris Minor and in Coventry on the Alvis TA/350. He also drafted in the best of the engineers already resident at Longbridge. He began with a large car codenamed XC9001 and a

Issigonis with sketchpad, surrounded by technical drawings, behind his desk at Longbridge.

Several prototypes were built for XC9003. This one, pictured at Longbridge in 1958, has the sliding windows which would be a distinctive feature of the final design but, as yet, no boot lid.

mid-sized car codenamed XC9002. The smallest vehicle, XC9003, was not at the top of the list for development. Though the early prototypes resembled the later Mini shape, at this stage Issigonis dismissed the idea

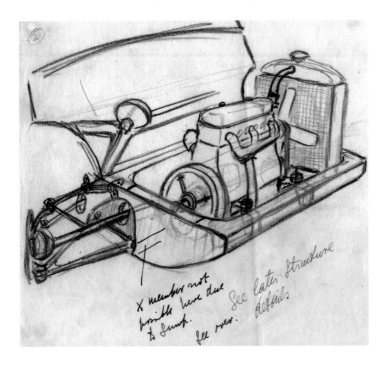

An original Issigonis sketch of the transverse engine arrangement, c. 1957.

11

The Issigonis team (top to bottom): Jack Daniels (key engineer on the Morris Minor), John Sheppard and Chris Kingham (from the Alvis project), Charles Griffin (Longbridge engineer), and Alex Moulton (freelance suspension specialist who also worked on the Alvis).

of front-wheel-drive as unworkable, even though he had already experimented with the concept on an adapted Morris Minor. The team had been working together for nearly a year when international politics unexpectedly intervened.

In 1956 President Nasser of Egypt nationalised the Suez Canal, the main route for the export of oil from the Middle East to Europe. In response, Britain and France mounted a botched military response. The result was a fuel crisis which put a premium on small, economical vehicles. In response, Leonard Lord personally instructed Issigonis to concentrate on the creation of a fuel-efficient small car to be put into production as quickly as possible. Austin and Morris had prided themselves on their performance in this sector of the market in the 1920s and 1930s – the Austin Seven and Morris Eight had both been market leaders. Lord was not happy about the sudden appearance of German 'bubble cars', which had gained a quick boost in the months following the Suez crisis. Though these cars never really presented much of a threat to mainstream industry, they caught his attention and prompted his decision to shift the company's product policy in this direction.

So Issigonis put the larger prototypes on one side in favour of the less-developed XC9003. The problem with the designs of many small cars, including the bubble cars so disliked by Lord, was that they were not really cars in the true sense of the word, unable either to seat four people or carry a reasonably sized power unit. Issigonis took a radical approach to eliminate these problems, calling on all of his experience to date. This encompassed not just the ideas developed during the Mosquito and Alvis projects, but also his youthful exploits with modified Austin Sevens and the Lightweight Special.

The objective was to build the smallest four-seat car possible – the final overall length would be 10 feet and half an inch – but at the same time to maximise the amount of space available to the driver and passengers without compromising the engineering. The breakthrough which made this possible was to fit the power unit sideways (or transversely) across the engine bay instead of the usual arrangement of lengthways (or in-line). Not only did this liberate space, it meant the car could utilise an existing power unit, the proven A-series engine, which was first fitted to the Austin A30 in 1951. The transverse configuration would eventually become the standard in small cars all over the world. In addition, Issigonis placed the gearbox in the sump under the engine using a shared oil supply. He returned to the idea of front-wheel drive, which gave more stability while minimising the transmission channel that intruded into the floorpan of a car. His collaboration with Alex Moulton produced an innovative rubber-cone suspension which greatly improved handling and ride. The addition of unusually small 10-inch wheels was the final touch.

Issigonis had a unique style of working through sketching rather than by verbal explanations to communicate his thoughts. He kept a continuous sequence of notebooks containing his ideas, which stretched back to the beginning of his career in the 1930s. For those who worked most closely with him, it was an exciting time. It was their job to translate his lateral thinking into workable engineering drawings and experimental prototypes. Those working at more of a distance – the draughtsmen in the drawing office for example, the production engineers and the marketing men – were less tolerant, often characterising him as an autocrat who would not listen to criticism and who treated others with arrogance and contempt.

As Lord had instructed, the work was completed in a very short timescale of three years, but keeping to his timetable came at a cost. XC9003 moved on from the experimental stage to the Austin drawing office, where it became ADO 15, ready for the final tooling drawings to

Early production in the Car Assembly Building (CAB1) at Longbridge. Though production was split between two sites at Longbridge and Cowley, Austin and Morris models were mixed together on the same lines.

NO SMOKING BEYOND THIS BOARD

This sectioned vehicle demonstrates the spaciousness of the ADO 15 interior. Note the upright driving position, 'magic wand' gearstick, optional tailored hamper under the rear seat, and 'de-luxe' two-tone vynide upholstery.

be prepared so it could go into production. There was, however, little demarcation between what was still experimental and what was final. Experimental drawings were being turned into tooling drawings at breakneck speed and the draughtsmen were not Mr Issigonis's biggest fans. The nickname 'Arragonis' was often muttered in the drawing office, as was the variant 'Issygonyet'.

The earliest production version of ADO 15, an Austin, was assembled at Longbridge at the beginning of April 1959. It was immediately subjected to a thorough test that revealed a frightening collection of faults. Work went on throughout the summer to diagnose the many problems which arose and to prescribe suitable solutions. To make things worse, even though manufacture had already begun, the testing programme had not been concluded. Prototypes and early production vehicles continued to be sent out on the proving grounds and public roads of Britain, and on extensive continental trips. This provided a dual opportunity to finish testing the car while showing it to dealers in potential export markets. The faults found during initial assembly, combined with the final test results, meant that details of the specification were being altered from week to week, continually pushing up the costs of manufacture. The situation was not helped by the fact that the ADO 15 was subject to a complex manufacturing process, split over a number of locations, including Longbridge, Cowley and several panel-pressing plants.

The car was launched in 1959 as an Austin and a Morris. These early brochures show how BMC tried to differentiate between the two badges with distinctive marketing campaigns, even though there was no fundamental difference between them.

Despite all the difficulties, the car was launched, as planned, in August 1959. It was a bold move on the part of BMC to link advanced engineering with mass-market sales. But the marketing campaign was hampered by corporate confusion over what the car represented and at which sector of the market it should be aimed. The shape and size of ADO 15 was so startling compared to anything else being sold by British manufacturers in 1959 that the senior management felt some nervousness about its styling. Deputy Chairman George Harriman therefore asked BMC's Italian design consultant, Battista Pininfarina, for his opinion and felt reassured when he declared 'It's unique, don't change a thing'. Unfortunately, this was not a view shared by the men in charge of the sales department, many of whom had been there since the 1930s and remembered Herbert Austin and William Morris personally. They were mostly traditionalists who disliked the car immediately for its unconventionality. Their reaction was much closer to Lord Nuffield's view of the Morris Minor ten years earlier, than to that of the Italian stylist responsible for their modern range of Farinas.

It made no difference what they thought of it, however; their job was to sell it. First of all, ADO 15 needed a product name, but 'Mini' was not the one chosen. In line with BMC product policy, it was to be launched under two separate badges – Austin and Morris. The car was aimed at the family market, so to provide continuity with the past it was decided to revive the two most famous small-car names associated with these marques: the 'Austin Seven' and the 'Morris Mini-Minor'. The reason that the word 'Mini' was sneaked into the Morris version was simple enough. The Issigonis Morris Minor was still at the forefront of the model range, so the 'Mini' would denote that this was a car in the same tradition but even smaller.

Differences between the Morris and Austin versions were only superficial. Each had its own grille design and badge, plus alternative sets of colour and trim options. Nevertheless, the publicity department went to great lengths to distinguish between them by producing separate press releases, sales literature and marketing slogans. The early promotional literature featured the car surrounded by a 'typical' family that appeared to carry an amazing amount of luggage round with them. Much was made of fuel efficiency and how easy it was to drive and park, especially for women. Yet, with a worrying lack of consistency, the marketing campaign also focussed on the car's technical innovation. The Morris Mini-Minor was labelled 'wizardry on wheels'. The Austin Seven was tagged 'the incredible Austin Se7en'. BMC believed pricing would be a key selling point. The early adverts boasted: 'ten feet long, but roomier inside than many an £800 saloon – yet the Austin Se7en is less than £500, tax paid'. Many of their competitors doubted whether they had taken enough care with their calculations to reach this conclusion on pricing.

The events put on to launch the car echoed this confusion about what audience they were trying to reach. The motoring press was treated to an exclusive preview on 18–19 August at the Fighting Vehicle Research and Development Establishment in Chobham, Surrey. This would give attending journalists the opportunity to experience the car's superior road-holding and handling for themselves. Issigonis attended in person and his charm and eccentricity proved to be a key element in the day's success.

A week later, the Exhibition Hall at Longbridge hosted an event for the non-specialist press, and this time the theme was its suitability as a family car. Perhaps because the senior sales team were so lacking in enthusiasm, BMC handed the task of organising this important occasion to Tony Ball, one of its younger sales executives. Although car launches in the 1950s were rather tame affairs, he persuaded his bosses to give him a substantial budget of over £500 for the day. He used it to stage a flamboyant show with a 'magic' theme to convey the excitement he wanted to generate. With the lights dimmed, a spotlight was shone onto a huge top hat in the middle of the stage and Tony Ball himself emerged from the gloom, wearing a magician's outfit and carrying a magic wand. At a wave of his wand, his assistants, dressed as showgirls, swung the top

In August 1959 Issigonis personally hosted a press day at Chobham in Surrey, where motoring journalists could experience for themselves the pleasure of driving BMC's 'baby' car.

hat open to reveal the Austin Seven inside. The audience held their breath as three tall men, two women and a child emerged, followed by two dogs. Once everyone was out of the car, they began to unload large quantities of luggage which had been packed into the multiplicity of storage spaces.

Journalists were positive in their reviews for BMC's 'baby' car, but this was not quick to translate into sales. Though curious drivers visited the dealerships to see what the fuss was about, they largely resisted the temptation to make a purchase. Both Issigonis and BMC had always seen the car as appealing to the family market, making a safe and pleasurable driving experience accessible to a wider range of the population, but potential customers were put off by the very basic level of trim and equipment that Issigonis had insisted on fitting, reflecting his own taste but not that of the ordinary motorist. They were concerned by the high tyre wear associated with the small wheels. They also seemed to agree with the BMC sales team that the car was just too unusual, so that they could not picture themselves either driving or maintaining it.

The launch event held in the Longbridge Exhibition Hall has just finished. Attendees crowd round the Austin Seven that sits in front of the giant top hat from which it emerged, along with the plentiful luggage used during the demonstration.

Even for those who overcame these reservations, continuing unreliability problems were another off-putting factor. One design fault in particular would hamper the early Mini and that was water leaks. It became apparent that the flanges of the floor assembly had been designed the wrong way round, allowing water to seep in whenever it rained, and this was only one of a number of routes which permitted wet conditions to find their way inside. This led to many jokes about driving in Wellington boots and keeping goldfish in the door-pockets. But the less amusing consequence was the damage it did to early sales and the expensive rectifications that wiped out the all-too-small profit margin.

By the end of 1960, the engineering problems had mostly been resolved, but at considerable time and cost and also at the inconvenience of early customers, who found themselves being drafted in as involuntary members of an extended testing programme. Meeting Leonard Lord's deadline had been an impressive feat, but it proved to be one with a huge price tag attached.

Publicity for the Morris Mini-Minor in 1961. Despite the date, the dress and hairstyles of the models – and their camera – show that the 'Swinging Sixties' had not yet begun.

A CAR OF ITS TIME

A T FIRST IT SEEMED AS IF BMC's expensive gamble had failed. Though the Mini did begin to sell after a hesitant start, sales figures throughout 1960 were nothing out of the ordinary, and the company appeared to have no coherent strategy for capitalising on their 'advanced engineering' venture, beyond putting vehicles on extended loan to motoring correspondents in the hope of getting some positive press coverage.

It was Issigonis's own influential circle of friends who put the car on the first step of its journey beyond the ordinary. His involvement with motorsport as a young man had been an excellent avenue to forming friendships with a number of socially influential people. One of these friends was society photographer Anthony Armstrong-Jones who, in 1960, married Queen Elizabeth's glamorous sister, Princess Margaret. The new Count and Countess of Snowdon took delivery of a very early model, which had been specially modified under Issigonis's personal supervision to accommodate Lord Snowdon's request that it would 'go quicker than anyone else's'.

Britain was changing in the 1960s. The early part of the decade is hard to distinguish from the post-war era in terms of attitudes and fashions, but gradually the culture of shortage and stoicism gave way to a strong desire to leave memories of the war and its consequences behind. The economy began to boom, and young people in particular wanted to enjoy themselves, rebelling against the restrictions of tradition, convention and class. The romance of the photographer and the princess epitomised a modern era when a commoner could marry into royalty. People took notice when the popular young couple took to the road in this unusual car. Before long, Issigonis was being asked to give the queen a drive round Windsor Great Park and, as the decade progressed, a whole host of people who were famous for very different reasons became fans: the Beatles, Twiggy, Peter Sellers, Marianne Faithful, Christine Keeler – suddenly, it was *the* thing to have.

In a way that has probably not happened before or since, BMC's baby car not only developed its own market, it created its own identity. In a further example of how far off-target the launch sales campaign had been, an increasingly

Opposite: To move the Mini upmarket, two more badges – Riley and Wolseley – were introduced aimed specifically at women. Advertising for the Riley Elf (a Mark III version from 1967) suggests sex and glamour, despite the dull grey duotone livery of the car itself.

enthusiastic consumer base abandoned the clumsy and deliberately old-fashioned labels Austin Seven and Morris Mini-Minor and simply called it the Mini. On 19 January 1962 the press office issued the following statement on an Austin letterhead: 'In view of the popular usage of the word *mini* when referring to the current Austin Seven model, it has now been decided officially to rename this model and its derivatives the Austin Mini.' In September 1967, when the Mark II version was introduced, the Morris Mini-Minor followed suit, being renamed the Morris Mini.

The very basic trim and style adopted by Issigonis on the standard Mini was not to everyone's taste, so from an early stage there were more luxurious versions of the saloon for those customers who did not share the Issigonis asceticism. The Mini Super-de-luxe provided a superior standard of trim. Two additional badges were introduced – the Wolseley Hornet and Riley Elf – both with a more

The sales department never went to unnecessary effort. The 1962 brochure which introduced the new 'Austin Mini' badging was exactly the same as the 1959 brochure, except for the slogan.

Lord Snowdon and Princess Margaret in a customised Mini. It carries several non-standard features, including an 'Austin Mini' bonnet badge, combined with a Cooper grille.

nimble and
luxurious

the

AUSTIN
SUPER MINI

This 1962 BMC
brochure for the
'Austin Super Mini'
is finally waking
up to
contemporary
trends. The
out-moded
'Seven' tag has
been dropped,
while the elegant
lady, and her
thoroughbred dog,
match the new
slogan 'nimble
and luxurious'.

elaborate exterior shape and upgraded equipment as befitted their sales slogan: 'the most luxurious small car in the world'. Though they suited the era in their own way, ironically they would do what the Mini never did, which was quickly to go out of date, and they were dropped after eight years on the market.

These offerings did not go far enough for a few wealthy customers who were prepared to pay for expensive conversions, some undertaken by independent coachbuilders like Radford or Hooper, others performed at the Longbridge factory. The less well off also wished to imprint their

The Riley Elf's
sister, the
Wolseley Hornet
(a Mark II version
from 1966) is
shown here on
a country lane
in Cornwall.

23

Before the Mini Cooper: three Morris Mini-Minors outside the BMC Competitions Department in Abingdon, about to depart for the 1961 Monte Carlo Rally. The team members, who are dressed very differently from the modern rally driver, all retired without finishing.

own individuality on their Mini and, ironically, its starkness made it the perfect medium for personalisation. There was a roaring trade in accessories and conversions, a trend which would only get stronger as the Mini grew older. 'I love *my* Mini' would be the mantra of the 1960s and 1970s, and it was not only the rich and famous who re-tuned their engines for extra performance. It became increasingly fashionable to attach the prefix 'mini' to everything from clothes to household goods. The miniskirt, popularised by fashion designer Mary Quant, was the most famous and enduring example.

Celebrity endorsement gave Mini sales the boost needed, but the road to iconic status would be cemented by its entry into the prestigious arena of motor sport. Issigonis had drawn on his youthful enthusiasm to create a vehicle which was easy and fun to drive. One of his favourite sayings was 'I come from a racing background – my idea of a car that handles properly is car that has wheels at each corner.' Thus, unintentionally, he endowed his mainstream family car with all the qualities necessary in a successful competition car. Amateurs began to race and rally the car within weeks of its launch. One of the earliest experiments was carried out by Daniel Richmond, a talented engineer who ran the Downton Engineering Works, which took its name from the small village of Downton near Salisbury in Wiltshire, where it was based. As well as tuning cars for an impressive list of important customers, Downton Engineering also prepared its own cars for specific races to enhance the reputation of the company. During the winter of 1959, when Mini sales were still struggling, Richmond created his first 'Downton' conversion from a basic Austin Seven. Though it did not win, it made an impressive showing during 1960 and attracted considerable attention in the motoring press.

The BMC competitions department was not far behind Daniel Richmond in adopting the Mini as part of its armoury. Competitions had been established at the MG factory in Abingdon in 1955 by John Thornley, who was General Manager of MG Cars and another one of Issigonis's old acquaintances from the race track. The department's brief was to use not just MG cars, but any suitable vehicles from the entire model range. BMC entered six Minis in the 1960 Monte Carlo Rally, and the results were respectable if not spectacular, with four cars finishing and a highest placing of twenty-third overall. Other rallies were producing similar results. Their efforts convinced them that the Mini had the potential to be an excellent competition vehicle. What hampered them was that its 850 cc engine did not develop sufficient power to make it an outright winner.

Back in 1946, when Issigonis and George Dowson entered the Lightweight Special in the Brighton Speed Trials – a 1-kilometre dash down the seafront along Madeira Drive – they found themselves up against John Cooper in

The power of association: a photoshoot for the first Austin Cooper sales brochure at Goodwood in April 1961. A Cooper racing car is carefully positioned and Bruce McLaren stands far left. An Austin badge and grille were superimposed at artwork stage.

his 'Cooper 500', which narrowly beat them over the distance. By 1960, Cooper was a Formula One team owner with two world championships to his name and he noticed the Mini's popularity with his drivers, Jack Brabham, Bruce McLaren and Roy Salvadori. George Harriman replaced Leonard Lord as chairman of BMC in 1961, and Cooper asked his old friend Issigonis to assist him in persuading Harriman to lend the Cooper Company a Mini. He fitted the car with the more powerful 997 cc A-Series engine that BMC was supplying for use in his Formula Junior car, added disc brakes and a remote gear shift, and brought the improved car back to Longbridge for a demonstration. Though sceptical at first, Harriman was eventually persuaded to market a Cooper version of the car, thus associating it in people's minds with Formula One success. In return for lending his prestigious name and assisting with development, John Cooper would get a royalty of £2 per car.

The first Mini Cooper appeared in 1961 and would become one of the most successful rallying and racing cars of the decade. Pat Moss, sister of Stirling Moss and one of the BMC works team's leading drivers, gained the first overall win in a Mini Cooper at the Dutch Tulip Rally in May 1962. John Love followed this on the race track by winning the National Saloon Car Championship in September 1962. The key to the Mini's domination

When Paddy Hopkirk gained the first Monte Carlo victory in 1964, the winning Mini Cooper and its drivers featured on *Sunday Night at the London Palladium* with famous stars of the day, including host Bruce Forsyth and comedian Tommy Cooper.

Ferrari 64

of motor sport would be the introduction of a variety of engines from which the competitor could choose, beginning with the introduction of the Mini Cooper 'S' in April 1963, offering the option of an uprated 1071 cc engine alongside the 997 cc version. In 1964 this contributed to victory in the European Touring Car Championship for Warwick Banks. More famously, it also led to the first outright Monte Carlo victory for Paddy Hopkirk.

The Mini Cooper would enjoy great success in all the rallies and race events on the sporting calendar, but it would become most famous for its Monte Carlo Rally victories. Held every January, this was the only rally to take place in the depths of winter. Cars set off from different starting points all over Europe. After two days' hard driving through ice and snow, the competitors would converge in France to follow a common route to their destination in Monaco. Although other rallies offered tougher driving conditions, none of them was as glamorous or high profile as Monte Carlo. Paddy Hopkirk's 1964 victory hit the front pages of every British newspaper and the winning car was photographed in Paris with the Beatles before being shipped back to Britain to appear on the peak-time TV programme *Sunday Night at the London Palladium*.

Enzo Ferrari sent Issigonis a signed picture of his visit to Maranello in 1964, where the friends posed with Ferrari's personalised Austin Mini Cooper.

In 1967 Rauno Aaltonen and co-driver Henry Liddon provided the BMC works team with its third and final Monte Carlo victory for a Morris Mini Cooper 'S'.

Inside the Competitions Department garage at Abingdon in 1966, mechanics work on the BMC team vehicles, which include Mini Coopers and MGBs.

As the car became ever more successful, the racing and rallying programmes became an irresistible force. Downton Engineering continued to tune cars for special customers such as the Aga Khan, Steve McQueen and Enzo Ferrari. The official BMC-sponsored Mini Coopers were being joined by a host of private entries from amateur motorsport enthusiasts who had adopted the Mini as their car of preference like the pre-war Austin Seven before it.

The official works team enjoyed a string of further successes. Timo Makinen won at Monte Carlo in 1965, but then, in 1966, BMC was robbed of its best ever result, a one-two-three for works drivers Timo Makinen, Rauno Aaltonen and Paddy Hopkirk. The Mini Coopers were controversially disqualified amid accusations that the lighting was illegal. The British press and public were convinced that the French authorities, jealous of the success of the little British giant-killer, had trumped up the charge to allow a French Citroën to triumph. Despite the initial disappointment of the disqualification, the actions of the French authorities proved to be counter-productive. The declared winner, Toivonen, accepted his prize unenthusiastically, talking of 'a hollow victory' and the disqualified cars arrived back in Britain to even more fuss than the previous two winning cars. The following year the BMC works team returned to Monte Carlo and took their final victory with the Mini Cooper, this time with Rauno Aaltonen at the wheel.

The success of the sporty Cooper reflected back onto the ordinary Mini and did a tremendous amount to boost its popularity. This worked together with the growth of celebrity culture to lift the Mini onto a different level from many contemporary products as an aspirational car. Though other cars such as the Ford Anglia, Triumph Herald or Hillman Imp would provide strong competition, in the long term they were unable to match the aura that the Mini was beginning to acquire.

Almost a decade after the original launch, publicity for the Morris Mini Cooper S Mark II shows that BMC's view of its target owner had changed considerably.

BUILDING ON THE MINI PHENOMENON

IRONICALLY, THE CAR THAT had been intended to widen access to motoring had found success as a symbol of an increasingly affluent post-war world, in which young people wanted to assert their independence from their elders and break away from post-war austerity. This does not, however, mean that the Mini failed to reach a wider market. Second-hand sales in particular put the car in easy reach of many new drivers. As Mini sales gained momentum, its presence on the road became ever more widespread. Driving schools adopted it to teach their pupils, the Automobile Association used Mini vans to replace their motorcycles and sidecars, and Mini post office vans and police panda cars became a common sight.

Alongside the standard saloon, BMC produced a number of variants to widen the car's appeal. An estate version – the Austin Countryman and Morris Traveller – was introduced in 1960. This mimicked the coachbuilt estate version of the Morris Minor, which was constructed on a wooden frame, though in the case of the Mini, the timber panelling was purely cosmetic. This feature seems to have been aimed at the English 'country' set, while the subsequent all-steel option without the panelling was directed at export markets. The estate offered an extra 4 inches of length, with more rear overhang than the saloon, as did the van and pickup that were introduced the same year. The van was particularly popular because it attracted a lower rate of purchase tax and yet, after a period of time, permission could be sought to fit windows in place of the rear panels and install a rear seat conversion. This created an economical and practical everyday vehicle at an affordable price.

The Mini automatic that first appeared at the end of 1965 was also groundbreaking, and particularly popular with disabled drivers who had so far been offered few choices at the lower end of the model range. It was fitted with a special gearbox which, in contrast to the three-speeds of most contemporary automatics, offered a responsive four-speed transmission with manual override. It was the first of its type to be designed and manufactured in Britain, a joint venture between BMC and Automotive Products of Leamington Spa.

Opposite:
The Innocenti factory in Milan, 1968. The Italian firm built Minis and 1100s under licence from BMC. Both of these are visible in the assembly hall, which is rather less crowded than its Longbridge counterpart, due to a lower volume of production.

In 1963 the Automobile Association replaced the motorcycles and sidecars used by its patrol services with Mini vans.

Issigonis continued to develop the Mini theme. There were still two vehicles left in the original model range which had been in process when the Suez crisis intervened to change priorities. XC9002, which became ADO 16, was launched in 1962 as the 1100. Slightly larger than the Mini, the 1100 was even more heavily badge engineered, with Austin, Morris, MG, Wolseley, Riley and Vanden Plas variants. The original design of 1955–6 was revised to follow the transverse engine with front-wheel-drive configuration. It was also the first car to feature the Hydrolastic interconnected fluid suspension system developed by Issigonis and Moulton, which had not been ready in time for ADO 15. The final flourish was styling by Pininfarina. Its elegance and driveability gave it wide appeal, and it became the best selling family car of its day in the UK. In some ways, it would occupy the market position that the Mini had originally been aimed at.

A family sees how many plants it can fit into its Morris Mini-Minor Traveller on a visit to the garden centre in 1960.

An automatic Mini with sliding doors in the design studio, c. 1967. The passenger seat has been removed to accommodate a wheelchair, allowing its occupant to slide easily into the driving position. Sadly, this ingenious adaptation did not reach production.

XC9001 was likewise remodelled as ADO 17, to be launched in 1964 as the Austin/Morris 1800, followed by a more stylish Wolseley version; but, though it offered vast amounts of interior space, the idea seemed a little redundant on such a large car. This time, Issigonis insisted on interfering with the Pininfarina styling and imposed an overly basic level of trim, inappropriate for a car aimed at the luxury end of the market. Unlike the 1100, the 1800 failed to hit the mark and sales never reached the levels anticipated.

The 1100 was as innovative as the Mini itself. It used the transverse engine with front-wheel-drive layout, while incorporating a new Hydrolastic suspension systems developed by Alex Moulton (left) and Alec Issigonis (right).

33

By 1966, Issigonis had completed his model range based on Mini principles. The whole Austin family is here — (left to right) the Mini, 1100 and 1800.

At the same time, work continued to improve the Mini itself. Though the distinctive shape, which had once sent shivers down the spines of the sales department, was now not only accepted but fundamental to its appeal, during its first decade there would be notable technical advances. In 1965 Hydrolastic suspension was added to the saloon. The Mark II version of 1967 included a larger back window and revised grille, while a 998 cc version was added to the basic range. The Riley Elf and Wolseley Hornet were given wind-up windows, but Issigonis, who had been promoted to BMC technical director in 1964, considered sliding windows to be superior and made it his business to stop them from being removed on any of the other versions. The unfortunate Lord Snowdon would find himself on the receiving end of this eccentricity after returning one of his cars to the factory for special tuning, only to find on its return that the wind-up windows he had paid to be added in had been removed. When he confronted Issigonis on the subject, he was told that it had been done 'to protect Margaret's hair, dear boy'.

ADO 34 was an attempt to create a two-seater, fitted with an upgraded Mini Cooper engine. Two prototypes were made – a hard-top and a soft-top –and sporty body-styling by Pininfarina was later added. The format seemed somehow inappropriate on a car whose ethos had been to provide a four-seater for the common man or woman and BMC dropped the idea. Other specialist car builders were less easily dissuaded. Cabriolet conversions were popular and many one-off sports versions based on Mini running gear appeared. Some companies produced their own variants in greater quantity, often in kit-form to avoid purchase tax. The Mini Marcos was a notable

A design drawing showing the Pininfarina body styling for ADO 34, one of many BMC efforts to adapt the Mini design which never reached production.

example of the genre. Created by Marcos Cars of Wiltshire, the Mini mechanicals were fitted with a glass fibre body/chassis unit and it proved very successful in competition because of its lightness.

The Mini Moke was initially thought of as a military vehicle, but its wheels were too small and its ground clearance insufficient for military purposes. As so often with BMC, the company seemed unsure where to aim the Moke, which never really found a role in the model range. It eventually became a leisure vehicle, built and sold in limited numbers. Even so, it enjoyed a lengthy, if complicated, career. Manufacture began in Britain during 1964, production was subsequently moved to Australia in 1968 and then Portugal in 1981, where it ended in 1996. There were several attempts to develop the Moke into something more serious, including a twin-engined version and, in the late 1970s, an Australian experiment with four-wheel drive, but essentially it remained a rather impractical runabout for hot climates. It nevertheless did make its mark on popular culture and enjoyed bit-parts in the *James Bond* films as well as the 1960s cult TV series *The Prisoner*.

The Mini Moke was another variant which did reach the market. This 1989 brochure from Austin Rover France illustrates its eventual fate as a 'fun' runabout.

As 1968 approached, BMC was offered an even bigger opportunity to feature its star car alongside such big box-office names as Michael Caine and Noel Coward in *The Italian Job*, a film which has become almost as iconic as the Mini itself. From the film-makers' point of view, it was unfortunate that production began just as Harold Wilson's Labour government decided to take an interest in Britain's struggling motor industry. Towards the end of 1967, Wilson strongly encouraged

PARAMOUNT PICTURES PRESENTS AN OAKHURST PRODUCTION

It's daylight robbery!
How do they get away with it?

MICHAEL CAINE
& NOEL COWARD
DO
THE ITALIAN JOB
ALSO STARRING U
NY RAF TONY ROSSANO
LL VALLONE BECKLEY BRAZZI
AND MAGGIE BLYE
WRITTEN BY TROY KENNEDY MARTIN
MUSIC BY QUINCY JONES
PRODUCED BY MICHAEL DEELEY

A poster depicting scenes from the 1969 film *The Italian Job*, which would help cement the Mini's reputation.

the two biggest remaining manufacturers – the Leyland Motor Corporation (which included Rover and Standard Triumph) and BMC (now part of British Motor Holdings along with Jaguar and Pressed Steel) – to negotiate a merger. The British Leyland Motor Corporation was incorporated in May 1968 and it was hoped this would improve the industry's chances of competing successfully, not just with continental manufacturers, but with emerging competition from Japan. George Harriman, in poor health, stepped down and Leyland's chairman, Donald Stokes, took the helm.

These developments were taking place during the making of *The Italian Job*, which was released on 2 June 1969. Only three cars in red, white and blue would appear on screen, but dozens of cars were required to complete the spectacular stunts. The company, preoccupied with its internal problems, decided it was not prepared to bear the costs just on the promise of some free publicity. Six Minis were sold to the production company at trade price and retail price was charged for the remaining thirty, but the film-makers found that the paint codes of the later deliveries did not match previous batches, causing them major problems with the continuity of shots. The chase sequences of the film were set in Turin and some scenes were filmed on the distinctive roof of the Fiat factory, whose chairman, Gianni Agnelli, provided complimentary Fiat Dinos and used his influence with the local police to stop the traffic in Turin for filming. He hoped to persuade the production company to go further by replacing the Minis with Fiats but, fortunately for the Mini, this would have made nonsense of the film's theme and the producers regretfully declined.

Issigonis was naturally proud of the role his creation played in the popular film and hired a cinema for a private viewing with some of his friends. The advent of British Leyland, however, marked the end of his years as the company's celebrity designer. His final design to go on the market (and British Leyland's first product) was the Austin Maxi, which proved to be a commercial disaster. Issigonis was moved sideways into research and development and Standard Triumph's chief designer, Harry Webster, took over as technical director. The Mini itself, however, continued to be hugely popular, both in the UK and overseas. In 1969 the two-millionth Mini was produced and the car reached its tenth birthday. To celebrate, the company held a major event at Silverstone to which all Mini enthusiasts were invited. Even if British Leyland had been tempted to get rid of the car so closely associated with its out-of-favour designer, it would have been hard for the company to ignore

Above and below: Mini owners paraded their devotion to the Mini at its tenth birthday celebrations in 1969. The slogan of the time could be seen as a warning to executives of the newly formed British Leyland not to tamper with their idol.

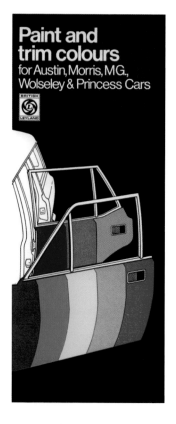

Paint and trim colours
for Austin, Morris, MG, Wolseley & Princess Cars

the slogan produced for the occasion: 'Don't play rough. I've got 2,000,000 Mini friends'. 1971 would be the year in which Mini production peaked with sales of 318,475 units worldwide.

The Corporation was in any case preoccupied with other sectors of the market and was concentrating its effort on two flagship projects which, ironically, would both be linked in different ways with the creator of the Mini. ADO 28 became the Morris Marina, aimed at the fleet car market. It was a rear-wheel-drive car which contained some elements of the Morris Minor, a tribute to the quality of a design which was now twenty-three years old. The other project was ADO 67, which became the Austin Allegro, a front-wheel-drive car whose engineering was based on the 1100.

It was necessary to keep the existing model range going until the new products were ready and in 1969 some key changes took place. Sensibly, UK Mini production was concentrated at Longbridge, doing away with the expense of running duplicate production lines at two different locations. Perhaps the most significant move was to drop the Austin and Morris badges in an effort to move away from badge engineering. The result was that 'Mini' was no longer just a model name – it became a brand in its own right.

Issigonis had already instituted a cost-saving programme which became ADO 20, and it fell to British Leyland to implement it as Mini Mark III. The bodyshell was re-engineered

Right: The Mini Clubman 1275 GT replaced the Mini Cooper. This 1979 version, complete with a pouting model clutching a race helmet, is painted vermilion red, one of an increasingly psychedelic range of colours made possible by new paints and chemicals. British Leyland's colour card from 1971 (above) illustrates a few more.

to make it simpler and cheaper to produce. Hydrolastic suspension was taken off the standard car and the earlier rubber cone system was reinstated. The visible door hinges were done away with. Now that Issigonis was out of the way, an effort was also made to introduce some long-needed refinements such as wind-up windows. It was hoped that these changes would make it possible to charge a higher price, making the car more profitable. At the same time, a new variant known as the 'Clubman' was introduced, featuring a squared-off front and initially retaining the Hydrolastic suspension. A revised dashboard replaced the distinctive central dial with a more elaborate set of instruments. The interior trim was also upgraded, though this did not serve to make the seats any more comfortable.

The Mini Clubman was launched before the standard versions of ADO 20 at the London Motor Show in 1969 so that it would appear more different from the Mini 850 and 1000 than it actually was. The Mini Cooper range was phased out over a period of three years, while the Clubman 1275 GT was brought in to take its place. This saved the company the £2 royalty, but lost it the prestige of the Cooper name. British Leyland made a further attempt to develop its own sports version when a Mini Clubman 1275 GT was sent to their current design partner in Italy to be modified as part of the ADO 70 or 'Calypso' project. The Michelotti studio added its own detailing to the design brief and three months later a rather different car was driven back, which must have caused some confusion among the customs officers who waved it through on disembarkation. Like ADO 34, however, the car did not reach production.

During the Leyland National Mini Championship in 1977 at Castle Combe, the Mini Clubman 1275 GT driven by Malcolm Leggarte crashes onto its roof in spectacular fashion.

Save Petrol PLEASE

Unfortunately for British Leyland, their mainstream product strategy, focussing on the Marina and Allegro, suffered a huge blow when another political crisis erupted in the oil-producing states of the Middle East during 1973. British Leyland was caught unawares as the Mini received an unexpected boost when another fuel shortage, combined with inflation, prompted people once again to trade down to small cars.

There were missed opportunities. BMC had entered into partnership with the Italian firm of Innocenti, makers of Lambretta scooters, in the early 1960s. At first, Innocenti produced Austin A40s under licence, but later moved on to Minis and 1100s, adding considerable flair to the basic trim of the car. They went a step further in 1974, bringing out the Innocenti 90 and 120,

Above and right: In 1972, Mini production reached three million. Executives George Turnbull, Filmer Paradise and Donald Stokes might have preferred to pose with their own design, but they proved unable to halt the company's decline, accelerated by another fuel crisis in 1973.

based on Mini subframes and mechanicals but featuring a 'hatchback' body, styled by Bertone. Though this seemed to reflect general trends in the market, British Leyland never seriously considered introducing the car to the UK and sales were confined to continental Europe.

As the Corporation's finances worsened, the British government, which had pushed for the merger,

decided to take a majority shareholding to save it from bankruptcy. It was reconstituted as British Leyland Ltd in 1975, its budget and product decisions subject to government approval from now on. The re-organised company struggled to find a coherent product plan as the 1970s drew to a close. Times were changing and rival manufacturers were beginning to bring out a series of 'super-mini' hatchbacks, based on the Mini layout but offering more refinement by increasing the size of the car. The Datsun Cherry, Fiat 127, Renault R5, Honda Civic and Ford Fiesta were leading examples. It was a market which BMC had pioneered and in which British Leyland was getting left behind.

An Innocenti brochure from 1974. The Mini 90 and 120 incorporated the increasingly popular 'hatchback', but, apart from on the unloved Maxi, British Leyland failed to take up the idea on their own model range.

A rail transporter with a batch of Mini Mark III cars departing from Longbridge in 1974. There is also a single representative of British Leyland's new hope, the Austin Allegro.

"Sit in one of the new Minis, you feel ten feet tall."

When we showed Eric Sykes a new Mini® Clubman 1100 he took a bit of convincing that it was a Mini.

The new contoured seats threw him. And the wall-to-wall carpeting. The new, easy-to-get-at controls didn't look like the last Mini Eric had seen.

And the fact that the new Minis are quieter, with an improved suspension for a smoother ride made it hard to convince him he really was in one of the most famous cars in the world.

But we did it in the end.

You see, the Mini's celebrated fuel economy hasn't changed. Neither has the larger than life feeling you get when you slide behind the wheel.

Try feeling ten feet tall at your Austin or Morris showroom. It's a great feeling. Ask Eric Sykes.

Welcome back to a better Mini.

Mini

From Leyland Cars. With Supercover.
® 'Mini' is a Registered Trade Mark of Leyland Cars.

THE GREAT SURVIVOR

F OR A MODEL to stay in production for a lengthy period, it requires
regular facelifts to keep up with the market. The question facing
British Leyland was whether it should continue to follow original Mini
principles or adopt the continental super-mini trend. Part of the company's
inertia stemmed from the belief that the original Mini was now too
firmly rooted in the national psyche to undergo radical change. The car
had retained its celebrity following and stars such as Twiggy, James Bolam
of popular TV show *The Likely Lads* and comedian Eric Sykes all participated
in renewed advertising campaigns. It also continued to be a very successful
competition vehicle. British Leyland sponsored its own Mini-based race
meetings and during the 1978–9 season a Mini Clubman won the British
Saloon car championships.

Ideas for a replacement had been in discussion for many years and,
surprisingly, one of the leading voices in favour of this was Issigonis himself.
He never intended the Mini to be his last word on the subject of small cars
and, as early as 1962, he was working on ideas for a successor. In 1967
he started to design a 'Mini Mini' which was intended to be even smaller
without sacrificing any passenger space. The key was a lighter, smaller engine
which became known as 9X. After BMC became part of British Leyland,
the 9X engine was dropped from the model programme and Issigonis
continued to develop his theme along an entirely different route, concentrating
as ever on underlying technology rather than superficial appearance. This
he did throughout the 1970s and 1980s, adapting a series of standard Minis
as prototypes for his development engines – and stubbornly replacing
the wind-up windows with his preferred sliding windows. Among these were
several gearless versions which used a larger engine and torque converter
to do away with the need for gears altogether.

British Leyland decided not to adopt his ideas, but they knew that
the Mini could not be kept going for ever. In 1972 the ADO 74 project
was started which followed the super-mini route with a wheelbase of 11 feet
6 inches. A second programme ran alongside, keeping more closely to

Opposite: Popular
comedian Eric
Sykes was among
the many
entertainers still
happy to endorse
the Mini. Though
the theme of the
1976 campaign
was 'a better Mini',
the only significant
change was
the option of an
1100 cc engine.

Left: Issigonis
reverses a 9X
prototype – his
proposal for a
replacement Mini –
on the drive of his
Edgbaston home.
It incorporated
the modern
'hatchback' feature
with improved
suspension and
packaging, while
welcoming back
sliding windows.

the original Mini concept, working with an overall length of 10 feet 6 inches. This developed ultimately into the ADO 88 project, led by members of the original Issigonis team. It was ADO 88 rather than ADO 74 which was finally adopted. The car was well advanced and about to go into production when Michael Edwardes was appointed the new chairman of British Leyland in 1977. He was unhappy with its lacklustre appearance and instituted a series of 'clinics' in which members of the public were invited to comment on the styling models. Their responses resulted in ADO 88 being halted, to be redeveloped as LC8. The length was increased to 11 feet 2 inches and the side profile of the car was stretched out so that it came closer, once

ADO 74 was
British Leyland's
first attempt to
design the type of
'super-mini' which
had become so
dominant by
the 1970s. This
mock-up was
displayed in the
styling studio, with
other design
sketches pinned to
the board behind.

ADO 88 adhered more closely to original Mini principles. This outline drawing compares its dimensions and packaging against the original Mini, ADO 15.

again, to the super-mini concept that rival firms had already adopted. As a result, the car's release was held back for a whole year.

To fill the gap, British Leyland embarked on renewed publicity for the Mini, holding a big party at Donington Park to mark its twentieth birthday, accompanied by the release of a limited edition called Mini Twenty. Though twenty-one might have been a more logical choice for celebration, the purpose of the event was to give Mini a boost as the public waited with bated breath for the launch of the much-delayed 'new' small car, LC8. This finally emerged onto the market the following year as the Austin mini Metro. Best remembered as simply 'Metro', it succeeded in revitalising UK sales in this important market sector.

In 1979 the basic Mini 850 was revised as the City. It included painted bumpers, cloth seat inserts, a side-stripe incorporating the new name and vibrant colours such as this 'inca yellow'.

It was believed that the Mini would now die of its own accord and the Clubman saloon was withdrawn in 1980, followed two years later by estates, vans and pickups. Yet, against expectations, the saloon soldiered on, its charisma apparently undiminished. As long as the car was producing respectable sales, especially overseas, the company was reluctant to wield the axe. No one, it seemed, wanted to be seen as the executive who killed the lovable Mini and it quietly returned to its original role as a niche car. In 1985 production reached the impressive landmark of five million, an achievement which was celebrated by TV personality Noel Edmonds, who at this period was retained as an ambassador for British Leyland's Austin Rover division at publicity events.

In 1979, Longbridge built a highly automated robot production facility for Metro bodyshells called 'New' West Works. The Mini line in 'Old' West Works continued in its shadow, persisting with the old hand-welding techniques.

Because of its stripped-down styling, the Mini did not look out of place as the shape of the vehicles around it changed. The two basic models were now named City and Mayfair, but the endless stream of limited editions continued with ever more quirky names and flamboyant colour schemes – Chelsea, Ritz, Piccadilly, Park Lane, Advantage, Red Hot, Jet Black, Flame, Rose and many more. Perhaps the most poignant was launched in 1988, the year of Issigonis's death. The Mini Designer was linked to

TV presenter Noel Edmonds shared a glass of champagne with the workforce to celebrate the production landmark of five million in 1986. The car was the more expensive Mayfair version, which had replaced the Mini 1000.

Mary Quant, the woman who had helped cement the car's fame by introducing the miniskirt.

The company was changing too. In 1986, British Leyland reinvented itself as Rover Group in an attempt to shake off the stigma of strikes and poor production quality associated with the old name. Then in 1988 Margaret Thatcher's Conservative administration succeeded in selling it back into private ownership when British Aerospace agreed to buy the government's shareholding.

As the years passed, the Mini saw no further engineering development but was sustained by a succession of anniversaries and nostalgic advertising campaigns which fed on popular affection. Building on the success of Mini Twenty, a regular series of birthday parties began, held every five years and always accompanied by the release of a limited edition. Each anniversary, the events got bigger and Mini lovers flocked to Donington or Silverstone to express their devotion and show off their personalised vehicles in ever more exuberant processions and displays. A sales brochure for Mini Forty even played a tinny version of Happy Birthday when it was opened.

The *Mini Designer* of 1988 was one of many limited editions which reminded people of the Mini's illustrious past. It is pictured with Mary Quant outside her shop in Carnaby Street, London.

As the 1990s dawned, the Mini's iconic status was, if anything, becoming more entrenched. In 1991 the magazine *Autocar & Motor* voted it the 'greatest car of all time' and in 1995 its successor *Autocar* named it 'car of the century'. The high performance Mini ERA turbo, based on a heavily modified City bodyshell, was produced between 1989 and 1991 and the Mini Cooper itself made a return in 1990. Originally introduced as a limited edition, it soon resumed its place as a regular model, even making an appearance at the Monte Carlo Rally, driven by Paddy Hopkirk with 'retro' number plates but a distinct lack of success. It also continued to make regular appearances on TV and in film and not just in dramas about the 1960s. A Mini took the starring role in the 1981 Australian road movie *Goodbye Pork Pie* and later featured in the 1994 hit *Four Weddings and a Funeral* and the 2002 blockbuster *The Bourne Identity*, among others.

There were a number of ventures to produce Minis abroad over the years, in Europe and beyond. One interesting example was the plastic or glass-fibre Mini. The intention was to create a bodyshell for manufacture in

Right and below:
Promotional
campaigns on
television and on
billboards blatantly
played the
nostalgia card.
In 1989 Twiggy
was drafted in
to film an advert
(directed by
Sixties photograph
er David Bailey)
for the Mini Thirty
limited edition
with the tag line;
'you never forget
your first Mini'.

overseas territories which did not have access to either the materials or
the facilities needed for the more usual pressed steel bodywork. In the late
1960s the Pressed Steel Fisher plant at Cowley undertook significant research
into the concept and tested a running prototype. Efforts to translate this into
manufacture at British Leyland's Chilean plant did not meet with success.
The idea was revived in 1990 when one of the original prototypes, which had
survived as part of Rover Group's heritage fleet, was sent to Venezuela for
evaluation as part of a collaborative venture with a local manufacturer. The
outcome was the Mini Cord, which started production at the Facorca factory
located in Mariara, Carabobo State, in December 1991. The mould included

The structure of the Mini Cord bodyshell looks like something out of a science fiction movie.

The 'moving' assembly line of the Venezuelan factory was less futuristic, consisting of trestles on wheels. The workforce does not seem to consider the face-masks, provided to protect against inhaling toxic irritants, as essential equipment.

fake seams around the roof to maintain the Mini's familiar appearance, while mechanical components and 998 cc power units were supplied from the UK. There was even a Cooper version, but output did not live up to expectations. Projections of up to five thousand units a year translated, in reality, to the production of 798 cars in 1992, which unfortunately proved to be the peak. Mini Cord remained a curious experiment, brought to a close in 1995.

MINI IN THE NEW MILLENNIUM

A S THE DECADES PASSED, it became increasingly difficult to get the Mini through all the safety and emissions legislation, even though its age entitled it to a number of exemptions. Though there had long been options to fit bigger wheels, these now became standard. The slight 'lip' which had been introduced around the wheelarches in 1984 became very pronounced on models fitted with the sportspack option, which included 13-inch wheels, affecting the purity of line inherent in the original bodywork. Nevertheless, the stream of limited editions continued and celebrities were as keen to endorse it as ever.

When BMW bought Rover Group from British Aerospace in 1994, they quickly recognised that the longevity of the Mini sprang not simply from the product, but from the strong brand identity which had grown up around it: the pull of the Mini name itself. They decided to make it a major part of their future plans, initiating the R50 project, which was presented to their marketing team in the following terms:

> to create a worthy successor to the current Mini and, in doing so, maximise the opportunities presented by such a powerful and emotive brand name and exploit the business opportunity presented by an emerging premium small car sector brought about by changing consumer attitudes and behaviour.

Part of the investment programme took into account the considerable cost required to keep the existing Mini in production until the turn of the millennium, when the new model would be ready. In 1996 BMW undertook a major facelift which included an airbag, a revised front radiator and impact beams. To recoup some of the cost of keeping it on the market, the price of the standard Mini rose dramatically from around £6,000 to £9,000. Yet it kept selling, regardless. When the Metro, rebranded by BMW as the Rover 100, went out of production at the end of 1997, still the Mini lived on. This only strengthened BMW's conviction that the Mini name was one of

Opposite: In October 2000 the press were invited to witness the end of Mini production at Longbridge. Sixties pop singer Lulu drove the final car out of CAB1 to the cheers and tears of the workforce.

the most valuable assets that they had acquired. Marketing campaigns continually used the words 'individuality', 'emotion', 'charm' and 'fun'. Paul Smith, Kate Moss and David Bowie were each invited to design their own individual versions in 1998, and the following year a Paul Smith limited edition model went onto the market. The creation of a Mini brand back in 1969 had cemented the future of the car, even though British Leyland itself failed to recognise the significance of this decision.

The final chapter in the Mini story would be bound up with the fate of Rover Group itself. In 2000 BMW decided to refocus its efforts onto its

Opposite, top: In October 2000 press photographers crowd round the last of the 'Issigonis' Minis.

Opposite, bottom: In 1997 BMW displayed two Mini concepts – Spiritual and Spiritual Too – at the Geneva Motor Show, alongside a large picture of Issigonis, a signal that they intended to take the Mini name into the twenty-first century.

The remains of the assembly area in Longbridge 'Old' West Works, where Mini body-shells had once been welded, survived until the buildings were finally demolished in 2006.

traditional customers at the premium end of the market. The company was, however, intent on continuing with its plans for the new Mini, which represented a huge investment to date. Instead of setting up facilities at Longbridge as originally intended, production was switched to Cowley. Under a deal brokered by Tony Blair's Labour government, Rover Group, along with the Longbridge plant, was sold to the Phoenix Consortium led by John Towers. Part of the deal stipulated that the original Mini would be taken out of production on schedule, so it fell to Longbridge to mark the occasion at an official press event in October 2000. The last Issigonis Mini to leave the assembly line was a red and white Mini Cooper and, in a nod to the car's heyday in the 1960s, pop singer Lulu took the wheel to the strains of the *Italian Job* theme 'self-preservation society'. The car was donated to the British Motor Industry Heritage Trust and went on display at the Heritage Motor Museum in Gaydon alongside the first Morris Mini-Minor of 1959.

The first Morris Mini-Minor sets off from its home at the Heritage Motor Centre in Gaydon to join the 'Mini 50' birthday party in August 2009.

Even after its production run ended with a final total of around 5.3 million, the Mini continued to be voted at the top of polls by journalists, designers and the general public. It became one of a small number of cars that had such a strong hold on the imagination that its name and appearance came to be considered as powerful tools in a world market in which cars were becoming increasingly generic and lacking in individual character. As the twenty-first century dawned, several companies used the 'retro' theme to make their products stand out. Updated designs, drawing inspiration from the original Volkswagen Beetle and Fiat 500, would take to the road, but arguably the BMW MINI would gain the most success among the genre.

Nor has enthusiasm for what the Mini represents died. When Mini reached the distinguished age of fifty in 2009, an impressive parade of cars travelled from Cofton Park, opposite the site of the Longbridge factory, to the customary party at Silverstone, where young and old celebrated together the continuing affection in which the car is held.

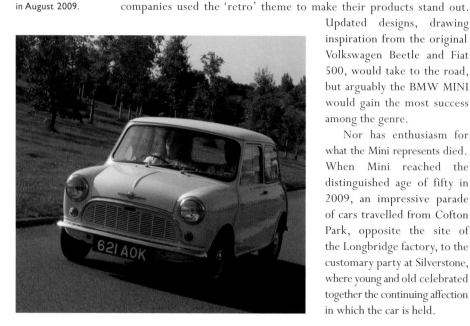

FURTHER READING

Bardsley, Gillian. *Issigonis, the Official Biography*. Icon Books, 2005.
Browning, Peter. *The Works Minis*. Haynes, 2005.
Campbell, Christy. *Mini, an Intimate Biography*. Virgin Books, 2009.
Field, Matthew. *The Making of The Italian Job*. Batsford, 2001.
Golding, Rob. *Mini Thirty-five Years On*. Osprey, 1994.
Moulton, Alex. *From Bristol to Bradford-on-Avon: A Lifetime in Engineering*.
    Rolls-Royce Heritage Trust, 2009.
Pressnell, Jon. *Mini, the Definitive History*. Haynes, 2009.
Rees, Chris. *Complete Classic Mini*. MRP, 2003.

PLACES TO VISIT

Heritage Motor Centre, Banbury Road, Gaydon, Warwick CV35 0BJ.
    Telephone: 01926 641188. Website: www.heritage-motor-centre.co.uk
National Motor Museum, Beaulieu, Brockenhurst, Hampshire SO42 7ZN.
    Telephone: 01590 612345. Website: www.beaulieu.co.uk
Haynes International Motor Museum, Sparkford, Yeovil, Somerset BA22 7LH.
    Telephone: 01963 440804. Website: www.haynesmotormuseum.co.uk
Atwell-Wilson Motor Museum, Stockley Lane, Calne, Wiltshire SN11 0NF.
    Telephone: 01249 813119. Website: www.atwellwilson.org.uk

HISTORIC MINIS

Many of the significant Minis mentioned in this book have been preserved at the Heritage Motor Museum. Just a few of them (as of 2013) are listed below:

Morris Mini-Minor, first production Morris, 1959.
Austin Seven, Downton conversion, 1959.
Mini Cooper 'S', Monte Carlo Rally winners of 1964, 1965 and 1967.
ADO 34, Pininfarina-styled prototype, 1966.
9X Mini, Issigonis prototype, 1969.
ADO 70, Michelotti-styled prototype, 1970.
Gearless Mini, Issigonis prototype, 1975.
Mini Cord, Venezuelan plastic body, 1992.
Mini Cooper, last production Mini, 2000.

INDEX